Literacy and Language
Anthology

3

Janey Pursglove and **Charlotte Raby**

Series developed by **Ruth Miskin**

OXFORD
UNIVERSITY PRESS

OXFORD
UNIVERSITY PRESS

Great Clarendon Street, Oxford, OX2 6DP,
United Kingdom

Oxford University Press is a department of the
University of Oxford. It furthers the University's
objective of excellence in research, scholarship,
and education by publishing worldwide.
Oxford is a registered trade mark of Oxford University
Press in the UK and in certain other countries

British Library Cataloguing in Publication Data
Data available

ISBN: 978-0-19-833075-2

10 9 8 7 6 5 4 3

Paper used in the production of this book is a natural,
recyclable product made from wood grown in sustainable
forests. The manufacturing process conforms to the
environmental regulations of the country of origin.

Printed in China by Imago

Acknowledgements

Cover illustration by Anaïs Goldemberg

Illustrations by: Laura Anderson; Barking Dog; Mark
Chambers; David Dean; Christiane Engel; Ben Galbraith; Anaïs
Goldemberg; Laura Hughes; Gwen Keraval; Andrew Painter;
Marcin Piwowarski; Stephano Tambinelli; Anthony Trimmer

The publishers would like to thank the following for the
permission to reproduce photographs: **p13**: LemonPrint/
Shutterstock; **p14l**: dmbaker/iStock; **p14r**: David Hughes/
Shutterstock; **p15t**: David Young/Shutterstock; **p15bl**: MarFot/
Shutterstock; **p15br**: Morag Fleming/Shutterstock; **p16t**:
Camping and Caravanning Club; **p16b**: omgimages/iStock;
p16-17: ciarada/Shutterstock; **p16-17**: Allaua/Shutterstock;
p17t: Mike Kemp/In Pictures/Corbis; **p17b**: Ant Clausen/
Shutterstock; **p18t**: David Lyons/Alamy; **p18b**: ScotShot/
Shutterstock; **p19t**: Image supplied by Haven Holidays; **p19m**:
MaszaS/Shutterstock; **p19b**: manzrussali/Shutterstock; **p31**:
Vadim Georgiev/Shutterstock **p47l**: lucekkk/Shutterstock;
p47r: notkoo/Shutterstock; **p54-55**: Piotr Zajc/Shutterstock;
p63: NASA; **p64-65**: NASA; **p65**: ESA; **p66**: NASA/JPL-Calech/
University of Arizona; **p67**: proxyminder/iStock; **p74t**: With
kind permission from Jamila Gavin/David Higham Associates;
p74b: With permission from Hachette Children's Books;
p74-75: Olga Drozdova/Shutterstock; **p74-75**: Eky Studio/
Shutterstock; **p75**: With kind permission from Jamila Gavin/
David Higham Associates; **p76**: With kind permission from
Jamila Gavin/David Higham Associates; **p77**: isoft/iStock; **p80**:
Colette3/Shutterstock

The authors and publisher are grateful to the following for
permission to reproduce copyright material:

Jamila Gavin p68 'The Enchantress of the Sands' first
published as 'The Witch of the Sands' in *Our Favourite Stories*
(Dorling Kindersley, 1997), copyright © Jamila Gavin 1997;
and **p76** opening extract from *Out of India* (Hodder Children's
Books, 2002), copyright © Jamila Gavin 2002, reprinted by
permission of David Higham Associates; **Andrew Fusek
Peters p52** 'Water Cycle' from *Leaves Are Like Traffic Lights* (Salt,
2011), copyright © Andrew Fusek Peters 2011, reprinted by
permission of the author.

We have made every effort to trace and contact all copyright
holders before publication. If notified, the publisher will
rectify any errors or omissions at the earliest opportunity.

The authors of the Fiction texts in this Anthology (excepting
those listed above) are as follows: **Jon Blake p4** *Sand Wizards,*
text copyright © Oxford University Press 2013; **Lou Kuenzler
p20** *A Tune of Lies* text © Oxford University Press 2013; **Roy
Apps p35** *A Tale of Two Robots,* text copyright © Oxford
University Press 2013; **John Dougherty p56** *Smash and Grab!*
text copyright © Oxford University Press 2013.

The authors of the Non-fiction texts (excepting those listed
above) in this Anthology are as follows: **Adrian Bradbury
p13** 'Your A to Z Holiday Guide'; **p16** 'Which Holiday?'; **p31**
'How to Make a One-string Guitar'; **p46** 'Nose in a Book or
Eyes on the Game?'; **p48** 'How Long Should Break Be?'; **p54**
'Where Does Water Come From?'; **p63** 'Wanted: A New Planet!'
text copyright © Oxford University Press 2013; **Charlotte
Raby p74** 'Jamila Gavin: Biography' text © Oxford University
Press 2013.

TEACHERS:
For inspirational support plus
free resources and eBooks
www.oxfordprimary.co.uk

PARENTS:
Help your child's learning
with essential tips, phonics
support and free eBooks
www.oxfordowl.co.uk

Contents

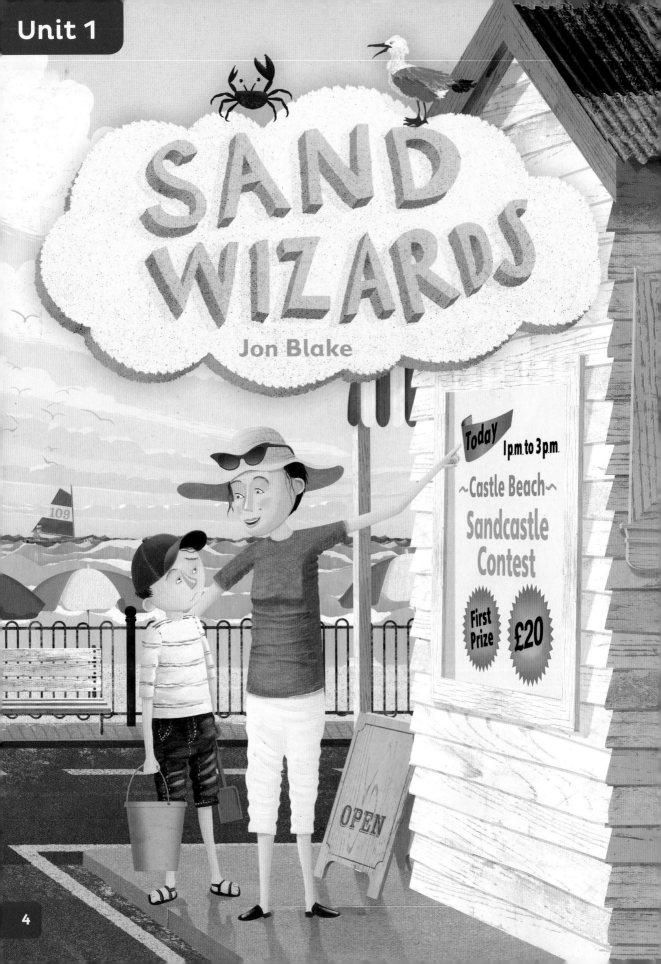

Cole's mum smiled at the poster:

Sandcastle Contest

First Prize – £20

"That will be perfect for you, Cole!" she said. "Why don't you have a go?"

Cole frowned. He knew he could build a great sandcastle. But it would be no fun doing it on his own.

"Just think what you could buy with twenty pounds!" said his mum.

Cole did think. He could buy a helicopter. Or a radio-controlled car. But he couldn't buy the thing he really needed. He couldn't buy a friend.

Cole tramped wearily across Castle Beach with his bucket and spade. The sky was grey, the holiday was nearly over, and everybody else was having a great time. It was so easy for everyone else to make friends. They knew how to act. They knew how to talk. They didn't have a **dark, depressing frown**.

Cole began to build his castle. He dug a deep moat and used the sand to build a tall mound. Slowly, the mound became a tower.

Suddenly, Cole became aware of someone watching. A scruffy-haired boy with pale lips and eager eyes. The boy seemed interested in Cole.

"That's good how you do that," said the boy.

Cole carried on building his tower. He didn't want to look at the boy.

"I had an argument with my brother," said the boy.

Cole ignored him, but the boy moved closer. "I can build castles," he said.

Cole knew what the boy meant. The boy wanted to join in. But why? What was his game? Did he mean to take over Cole's castle then chase him off?

Time wore on. The boy didn't go. He told Cole his name was Evan. "What's your name?" asked Evan.

"Cole," replied Cole.

"Cole," repeated Evan.

That was good. Evan hadn't called him Old King Cole or asked if he lived on a fire. Cole chanced a look at Evan, and saw that his face was open and friendly. But behind Evan was the huge grey ocean, just waiting to rush in and wreck everything.

"I've got shells," said Evan. He began to clamber down into Cole's moat. Cole was worried, but did nothing to stop him. Evan took shells out of his pocket and began pressing them into the tower.

"We need more near the top," said Cole.

Evan put more shells near the top. Cole watched for a while, then took a few shells himself.

"You've got to space them evenly," he said.

Cole showed Evan what he meant and Evan listened. The two boys settled down to work together. It gave Cole a good feeling.

"Have you got a brother?" asked Evan.

"No," said Cole.

"You're lucky," replied Evan.

They both laughed.

"This is going to be a brilliant castle," said Evan, a few minutes later.

"It needs a flag," replied Cole.

"I could get a flag!" said Evan.

"Where from?" asked Cole.

"I could buy one from the shop," replied Evan.

Cole couldn't believe that Evan would do this. But Evan clearly meant it. He counted out the money in his pocket then set off towards the entrance to the beach, where there was a row of shops.

"Look after our castle!" he called.

Our castle. That sounded great to Cole. The world suddenly seemed full of hope, and for a moment the sun broke through the clouds, turning the ocean a warm and friendly blue. Cole went back to building his tower with twice as much energy. It really was the best castle ever.

A few minutes passed, then a few more. Where was Evan?

Come on, Evan!

Cole did not want to lose his new friend.
He had to go and find him.

Cole's frown returned as he searched the beach
and the steps up to the shops.

Where *was* he?

Suddenly Cole's heart leapt. *There* he was – in the queue
for ice cream!

Time to say something funny.

"Double choc-chip for me, please!" cried Cole, jumping in front of his new friend.

Evan stared at him as if he were a complete stranger.

Then Evan turned his back.

Cole's ears burned with shame. He began to walk away, faster and faster, until he was running full tilt across the beach. What an idiot! What a stupid idiot, trusting that boy, thinking he'd made a friend. Cole would *never* make a friend. Never in his whole life.

The spade was stuck in the moat. Cole seized it. Then SMASH! He brought the spade down onto the castle. Again and again he smashed it.

Then there was a shout.

"Cole! Stop!"

Cole looked up. Evan was racing towards him. Not far behind Evan was another boy, a boy who looked exactly like Evan. In this boy's hand was an ice cream.

The boy from the queue!
"Why are you smashing up our castle?" asked Evan.
"Is that your brother?" asked Cole.
"Of course it is," said Evan. "Can't you see?"
Cole had never felt so stupid, or **so relieved**. **With a heart as light as a feather**, he began to rebuild the castle. With help from Evan, it was soon complete.

Naturally it won the contest, and Cole and Evan shared the twenty pounds. The money was gone in a week, but the friendship would last much longer.

Your **A** to **Z** Holiday Guide

A

Airport These days taking a plane can be as cheap as going by train. And it's much faster.

Anorak Knowing the British summer weather, you may want to pack one of these.

B

Bathing costume Bright colours are a must. Try canary yellow or shocking pink!

Beach ball Blow it up then bounce it on Dad's head while he's having a nap on the sand. Then run for it!

Bed and breakfast Cheaper than a hotel, and with friendly, personal service. An English speciality.

C

Camping Wake up to the sound of birds singing, cows mooing… and Dad snoring. (Warning: stay out of the way while Dad's struggling to put up the tent. Things could get nasty!)

Caravan A bit like camping, but with showers…and your mattress won't go down in the night!

Castles Britain is full of them. Great places to explore and learn about history.

Windsor Castle: one of Queen Elizabeth II's homes

Castle attractions

Some castles are used as venues for festivals and events. You can learn about Merlin and magic at Warwick Castle or go to one of the many festivals held in castles around the UK.

Castle ruins

Many ancient castles are crumbling ruins but you can still visit them and imagine what life in medieval times was like.

Duntulm Castle on the Isle of Skye in Scotland

Cream tea You can't go into the countryside without having one. Light-as-air scones with masses of clotted cream and jam piled on top.

D

Dartmoor Feeling energetic? Take a picnic and tramp up and down the hills. Stop to feed the famous Dartmoor ponies.

Dartmoor, in south-west England

E

Edinburgh Fancy a city break? Scotland's capital has everything you need: shopping, history, museums and nightlife.

Deckchair No beach is complete without these stripy sun-seats.

Disco You'll want one of these for evening entertainment.

A B C D E F G H I J K L M N O P Q R S T U V W X Y Z

Home	Budget	Special Occasions

Which Holiday?

What's **your** ideal holiday? Not sure? Well, we're here to help. Here are some ideas. Just click on the links for more details.

Camping

If you're an outdoor type, you'll love a camping holiday. Wake up to the smell of breakfast sizzling away on the stove, then settle down on the grass and tuck in. Enjoy walks and picnics in the beautiful British countryside.

Many family campsites have everything needed to make your holiday fun: pools, slides, amusements, games room, and shows and discos in the evening. After an active day, what could be better than to snuggle into yo lovely, warm sleeping bag? What's more, this holiday won't break the bar

The British weather can be unpredictable, though. You'll need to pack some waterproo clothes, and some board gam for those rainy days.

☞ **Click here for our selection of the best family campsites**

City Break

If camping's not for you, maybe you'd prefer the hustle and bustle of city life: the busy streets and the noise of traffic? If so, why not check into a hotel and enjoy the excitement of the big city? See the sights on an open-top bus tour, wander round museums and shop till you drop.

In the evening you can go to the cinema, or maybe visit a theatre and catch a show.

This is not a relaxing holiday, and can be expensive, so you may want to limit your stay to just a few days.

The UK's most popular city break destinations are **London**, **Edinburgh** and **Liverpool**.

Home   **Budget**   **Special Occasions**

Sun, Sea and Sand

The perfect mix! You can wear yourself out playing games on the beach and building sandcastles, and then cool off with a refreshing dip in the sea. Take a picnic lunch, and follow it with a yummy ice cream.

Many seaside resorts have a pier, with amusements and electronic games. Finish the day with a trip to the funfair, and fish and chips on the way home.

Temperatures in the UK can reach as high as 30°C or more in the summer, so make sure you pack your sun cream. Wind and rain are also common though, so don't expect to spend every day on the beach.

Follow this link to compare the UK's top 5 seaside resorts

Holiday Park

A holiday park is like all your destinations rolled into one. Drive through the gates and you'll find yourself in a world of shops, indoor and outdoor pools, amusements, shows, games and fun activities. No matter what the weather's like, you'll always find something to do.

Holiday parks are great places for making new friends. You can usually stay in chalets or caravans, so you can cater for yourself, but there are plenty of snack bars and restaurants too.

Most holiday parks are in seaside resorts, so you'll have easy access to a beach.

Costs can be high for a family of four or more, and you'll need to book well in advance.

☞ **Click here to find a holiday park and make a booking**

A Tune of Lies

Lou Kuenzler

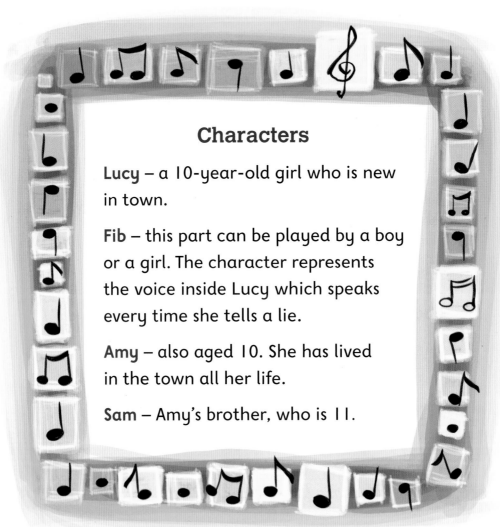

Characters

Lucy – a 10-year-old girl who is new in town.

Fib – this part can be played by a boy or a girl. The character represents the voice inside Lucy which speaks every time she tells a lie.

Amy – also aged 10. She has lived in the town all her life.

Sam – Amy's brother, who is 11.

Scene 1

It is summer. The scene takes place in a small park beside a row of terraced houses. The action begins halfway through a conversation where the children have begun to make friends.

Lucy It's lovely to have this little park right on the street where we live.

Amy *(On a swing)* It's great to have someone new to play with too. Before you moved in it was only me and Sam who ever came here.

Sam We're the only kids our age who live in the street.

Amy *(**Elated**)* And now we've got the whole of the summer holidays to play here.

Lucy Let's have a picnic or something. *(She points down the street.)* I can go home and get some food.

Amy Great idea.

Sam *(Checks his watch)* Count me out. I've got a music lesson at half-past.

Amy Sam plays the trumpet. He's only been playing a year, but he's amazing. What was it Mr Hammond called you?

Sam *(Grinning and pretending to bow to an audience)* A virtuoso!

Amy Basically, it means he's brilliant.

(Lucy is about to show she is impressed. But perhaps she is a little jealous too – or thinks that Sam and Amy are showing off – because instead of the answer she planned, Fib talks for her and a lie pops out.)

Fib I'm really musical too.

Amy Are you really musical, Lucy? You're so lucky. I don't play anything.

Fib Yes! *(Grinning)* I've been called a virtuoso too … lots of times.

(Lucy looks away, not making eye contact with anyone.)

Sam What instrument do you play?

Lucy Er…

Sam *(Excited)* You should bring it down to the park and we could make a little band. Amy can pretend to be the conductor.

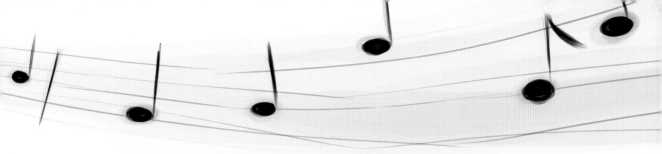

Lucy Er... I don't think so.

Amy Why not? No one round here will mind if we make a bit of noise. They're really friendly.

Lucy *(Almost as if she is going to tell the truth)* No. It's not that. It's just…

Fib *(Interrupting)* … it's just that the instrument I play is really big. I can't carry it to the park.

Sam If it's a piano, I've got a little keyboard you can borrow.

Lucy *(Truthfully)* No. It's not a piano.

Fib *(Grins with pride at being so inventive)* It's a harp!

Amy A harp?

Fib Yes. It's huge and heavy and very expensive. Mum says I'm not allowed to take it out of the house.

Sam I've never actually seen a harp.

Fib *(Getting carried away)* Mine's real gold. It takes up half the lounge.

Amy I'd love to see it. Can we come round to your house? You and Sam could do the band there.

Lucy Er... That might be tricky.

....

Scene 2

Later that evening, Lucy is looking into the bathroom mirror. She is talking to her reflection, played by Fib.

Lucy Why did I say all that stuff about being musical? I've never even played the recorder!

Fib   But the harp sounds really impressive.

Lucy Amy did think it was cool…

Fib   And Sam too.

Lucy I just wanted them to like me…and now it's so complicated.

Fib   But think how **astounded** they were when they heard you were going to play at a fancy concert in London – at the Royal Albert Hall.

Lucy Oh no! I even promised them tickets!

Fib   They're sure to want to be your friends now, though! You're a famous musician!

Scene 3

Two days later. Amy and Sam are in the park.

Amy (*Perplexed*) It's strange we haven't seen Lucy again. She seemed to really like the park.

Sam I suppose she has to practise for her big concert.

Amy It's a pity she's so musical. I'm looking for a friend to come along to the 'Have-A-Go Orchestra' with me.

Sam Is that the group Mr Hammond was talking about?

Amy Yes. It's a summer scheme run by the council. Anyone who's never played an instrument can come along and try out a couple.

Sam Sounds great.

Amy (*Dejectedly*) It's a shame Lucy won't want to come, though.

Scene 4

Outside Lucy's house. Sam and Amy are ringing the bell. Lucy is hiding behind the door with Fib.

Amy Lucy? Are you there?

Lucy *(Whispering)* I can't let them in. They'll see I don't have a harp. I'll be so embarrassed.

Fib Leave this to me. *(Opening the door a crack)* You can't come in. My mum's a world-famous author. We mustn't disturb her work. *(Lucy tries to pull Fib back.)*

Amy I thought she was a nurse…?

Sam It was her who asked us to call round.

Amy She said you'd been moping about. *(Kindly)* It must be hard not knowing anyone round here.

Lucy It is...

Fib *(Still holding the door half closed)* But mostly it's because of the concert. I'm practising so hard.

Lucy No! That's not true. It's... *(She pushes Fib out of the way and flings the door wide open.)*

Sam What?

Lucy Nothing. It's just... I want to tell you something.

Fib *(Pushing in)* I want to tell you more about the concert. After London, I'm going on a world tour. I'm going to play my harp in Paris and New York and...

Amy Wow! That's amazing.

Lucy *(About to cry)* But it's not true. I'm not…

Amy You're not going on a world tour?

Fib I am, but…

Lucy No! *(Pushing forward and holding the door closed against Fib.)* None of it's true. There is no world tour. No concert either. There isn't even a harp. I don't play an instrument. Look! *(She opens the door to show the lounge. Fib is cowering.)* It was all a big lie!

Scene 5

A week later. The children are eating a picnic in the park. Fib is crouched in the corner, sulking.

Amy *(Smiling)* It's a shame the 'Have-A-Go Orchestra' didn't have a harp!

Lucy *(Blushing)* But I did have a go on just about everything else. I like the drums best.

Amy And I like the guitar. Now we really can have a band!

Sam *(Chewing)* Not until I've finished this cake. It's delicious.

Fib *(Brightening and rushing back to Lucy)* I made it myself. I'm a brilliant cook. I won a children's cooking competition on television and everything...

Lucy *(Groans)* Only joking. The cake's from the baker's down the road!

How to Make a One-string Guitar

Musical instruments can be very expensive. Some very old violins are sold for millions of pounds! But you don't have to pay a fortune for a stringed instrument. Here's how you can make a one-string guitar for hardly any money at all.

You will need:

scissors

1 metre of strong plastic string

sticky tape

an adult with sharp craft scissors and a drill to help

2 litre plastic drink bottle

pencil

1 First, cut or peel the label off the bottle.

2 Next, cut a small, square hole in the side of the bottle. This should be about 15 cm up from the base. Get an adult to cut a slit in the bottle with craft scissors, then carefully make it into a window about 5 cm square.

3 While you've got your adult handy, ask him or her to make a 5 mm hole in the centre of the base of the bottle.

Tip for adults
You can do this with scissors, but it's better if you use a drill.

4 Fold your piece of string in half, and push the looped end into the bottle through the drilled hole. Keep pushing the string into the bottle until you can pull it out of the top. (This can be very fiddly. Just keep trying!)

Tip
For instructions 5 and 6, it's easier if you turn the bottle upside down on the table.

5

Put the pencil through the loop in the end of the string, then pull the loose ends tight to keep it in place.

6 Tie the loose ends into a big knot, as close as you can to the base of the bottle. You can cut off the extra bits of string, or tape them to the outside of the bottle.

7

Now twist the pencil round and round to make the string tight. Put your finger through the window in the side of the bottle to pluck the string and play a note.

Tip
If the edge of your window is sharp, stick some tape over to make it smoother.

8

By twisting the pencil, you can change the pitch of the note. If you practise you can play a tune!

A Tale of Two Robots

Roy Apps

"Callum!"

"What?" Callum glanced up **absent-mindedly** from his sci-fi comic and saw his mum standing in the doorway to his bedroom. Her hands were on her hips and there was a fiery glint in her eyes.

"Your room is a tip! How many times have I told you to tidy it up?"

"Thirty-three since last Sunday," replied Callum.

"Well, I'm not going to tell you again," his mum **fumed**. "If your room isn't spotless by tomorrow morning, I shall come in and do it myself!"

"Mum, please, no, you can't—" Callum cried out in alarm.

"I mean it, Callum," shouted his mum, before turning to go, and slamming the bedroom door behind her.

Panic struck Callum like a thunderbolt. He daren't let his mum loose in his room. For one simple reason: his room wasn't just his bedroom, it was also his *laboratory*.

Callum was an inventor.

And if his mum came in to tidy up all the half-eaten banana and ketchup sandwiches and unwashed socks, she would also try to tidy up all his inventing equipment, including his chemistry set, his collection of toilet roll middles and his screwdriver.

On the other hand, no way was Callum going to tidy up his room himself!

There was only one answer to the problem, Callum thought: he would just have to invent and build his very own room-cleaning robot.

All through the long, stormy night, Callum invented away with nuts, bolts, microprocessor units, swivel-action 180-degree lever systems and yoghurt pots. By the time dawn rose over the horizon, he had finished building his room-cleaning robot. It lay on his bed. He wired it up to his electricity-generating exercise bike and began pedalling like mad.

At first, nothing happened, then suddenly bright clusters of red and orange sparks started to fly off the robot's hands and legs, like a firework display gone crazy. The robot rose slowly but steadily, until it was sitting bolt upright.

Callum stopped pedalling and went across to detach the wires from the robot's feet. The robot took a quick look around, turned to Callum and said: "Your room is a tip!"

"That's right," said Callum.

"Aren't you going to clear it up?" asked the robot.

"Certainly not," replied Callum. "You're the room-cleaning robot."

"Robert," said the robot, putting out a hand that Callum had made from bent barbecue skewers. "Robert is my name. Robert the robot."

Callum sighed and shook Robert's hand – carefully. "All right, Robert. Now clean my room. Please."

"OK," said Robert.

Robert tidied up Callum's room until it shone like a TV chat show set. He carefully avoided all of Callum's inventing equipment, including his chemistry set, his collection of toilet roll middles and his screwdriver.

Every day Robert tidied up Callum's room and every day Callum's mum cooed and simpered and called Callum "my darling boy". But Callum didn't mind, because after every kiss, she made him a strawberry and ketchup milkshake. It was too good to be true, Callum thought.

He was right. One Friday morning, Callum was just dashing out to school, when he almost bumped into Robert, standing by the front door.

"What are you doing?" Callum asked him, **tentatively**.

"I'm coming to school with you," said Robert.

"You can't!" exclaimed Callum.

"Don't try to stop me," replied Robert, with a pout of his metallic mouth. "'Cos if you do, I won't tidy up your room tonight. Or any other night!"

Callum knew when he was beaten.

"There's a new face in Red Class this morning," said Ms Shelley, Callum's class teacher. "Everybody, this is Robert."

Everybody in Callum's class turned to stare at Robert.

Ms Shelley sighed. "Red Class! There's no need to sit there like goldfish with your mouths all open, gawping at Robert. Now face the front, please."

At break time, everyone crowded
round Robert. They didn't talk to him,
but kept asking Callum questions.

"Why has he got a coat hanger sticking out of his
neck?"

"Because that's all I had to make his shoulders with,"
replied Callum **brusquely**.

"Can he exterminate people?"

"Of course he can't! He's only a room-cleaning robot,"
Callum snapped.

"He's well weird."

At that moment, Callum glanced up at Robert's face.
He could've sworn that the robot's metallic features
were somehow creased into an expression of sadness,
almost bordering on tears.

"Why don't you leave
him alone?" a girl's voice
piped up. It was Shannon,
one of Callum's classmates.
Everyone began drifting
away, leaving Shannon
alone with Callum and Robert. She took Callum to one
side. "I think Robert's lonely," she whispered.

"Don't talk stupid," said Callum, irritably.

"Why else do you think he came to school with you?
He's looking for a friend," retorted Shannon.

"He's got a friend," replied Callum. "Me."

"I mean," Shannon said, "a *robot* friend."

"Where am I going to find him a robot friend?"
protested Callum.

Shannon gave Callum a sideways look. "Come round
to my place, after school. And bring Robert with you."

"There," said Shannon, ushering Callum and Robert into the kitchen after school. "What do you think?" Standing by the sink was another room-cleaning robot!

Ignoring Callum and turning to Robert it said: "Hi, I'm Nita!"

Robert took a step back in amazement. "It's a *girl!*" he exclaimed.

"You have a problem with that?" asked Nita.

Callum gulped. "But… what… how…?" he stammered.

"You surely didn't think you were the only inventor in this town, did you?" asked Shannon.

Actually, that was precisely what Callum *had* thought, but he didn't think now would be a tactful moment to say so.

From that day onwards, Robert and Nita would often meet up for a chat. Of course, being room-cleaning robots they were happiest when they were talking about the dreadful state of Callum's and Shannon's rooms.

"You wouldn't believe the mess she left her room in this morning!"

"Try me! Do you know what I found under his bed last night? A mouldy cheese and onion crisp and a pile of toenail clippings…"

In fact, the more untidy Callum and Shannon left their rooms, the happier Robert and Nita seemed to be – it gave them more to talk about, after all.

And that suited Callum and Shannon just fine.

Nose in a Book or

Which would you rather do: curl up in an armchair with a good book, **or** settle down on the sofa with a computer game? **Is one** any better than the other?

If you listen to your teachers, they'll say reading books is far more useful. But are they right? There's no doubt that you can learn a lot from reading, especially if you choose non-fiction books. They're a great way to find out about the world.

Books can also be exciting, thrilling even. You may reach a stage where you're desperate to find out how a story ends — so desperate that you'll go without dinner or TV until you finish it.

Reading is definitely an important skill. You can't get by in life without it. People who read more are usually better speakers too. They have more words to explain themselves.

GERALDINE McCAUGHREAN

Peter Pan in Scarlet

The Official Sequel

Eyes on the Game?

However, books can take a long time to get through. It may take a week or more to reach the end. On the other hand, computer games can be over in a matter of minutes, then you can start all over again. Not only that, the latest games are even in 3D, and so lifelike that you almost feel you're inside the computer. What can match that thrill?

It's true that books are useful for information, but you can find out everything you need to know on the Internet.

Looking into the future, most jobs involve computers, so it's better to learn the skills at an early age.

To sum things up, it's clear that both reading books and playing computer games can give enjoyment. They can also help to develop skills that are useful throughout life. Maybe in an ideal world children should read books and play computer games.

How Long Should Break Be?

Characters

Sally, Matt, Joe and Eve are all Year 3 pupils.

Sally

Matt

Joe

Eve

In the corridor, about to go back into class after break.

Sally   Why are you looking so pleased with yourself?

Matt   We've just beaten the Year 4s at football, that's why!

Sally   Oh, whoopee. Big news! And what was the score in this epic match?

Matt   One–nil.

Sally   One–nil? Doesn't sound like much of a thriller.

Matt   Well, we didn't have very long to play, by the time we'd got the cones out of the shed for goalposts and sorted out the teams. Break times are way too short!

Sally   You're joking! My feet are like blocks of ice.

Joe   Why don't you play football with us?
That'd keep you warm.

Sally Well actually, Joe, not everybody wants to play games. Some people think that running around tires out your brain so you don't do as well in class. Anyway, not everybody's got lots of friends to play with. Some of us like to talk, or just chill, and we have loads of time for that. If we had shorter breaks, then we could go home ten minutes earlier.

Eve And do what? There's nobody to play with at home. It'd be boring.

Sally OK, but at least it's warm at home. Break times are freezing.

Eve Yes, but if they were any shorter kids wouldn't have time to put coats on in winter, would they? Besides, I run the snack shop. A shorter break would be a nightmare for me. We don't have enough time as it is.

Joe You're not kidding. Ten minutes I stood in the line for a cereal bar yesterday. When I finally got it and took the wrapper off, Mrs Taylor whisked it out of my hand and said: "Break time's over Joe, off to your Maths group." I didn't even get one bite.

Eve   I know what you mean, but it takes us time to set everything out and then put it away again afterwards.

Joe   So longer breaks would be better for everybody.

Sally   Excuse me?

Joe   Sorry – nearly everybody.

Sally   Hmm, except that schools that have longer breaks get worse test results. Fact.

Matt   Well, I still think it's a great idea. I'm going to suggest it to the School Council to discuss at their next meeting.

Sally   Er, I don't think so. Remember who the School Council member for our class is?

Matt   No, can't say I do.

Sally   Well, you're looking at her.

Matt, Eve and **Joe**   *Oh no!*

Water

Hot sun soak her up,

Cold cloud spit her out,

With a shout of thunder

How she falls.

Falls asleep, lies deep.

Mountains weep and dream

And in the dreams she seems to grow,

Stronger, longer,

Full of river-longing

Wide awake, thrills like a milkshake shivers,

She spills into the land.

But then a man-made hand stops her dead

With a dam.

Down, down, down underground, rushing round,

Pushed around by endless fists of metal, how she weeps.

Someone twists the tap.

Tap, kettle, cup of tea, into me and out of me.

Down the drain, underground, rushing round,

Spilling into land

And filling out the sea where the hot sun waits:

How she sings!

Andrew Fusek Peters

cycle

(A rhythm poem for acting out or different voices)

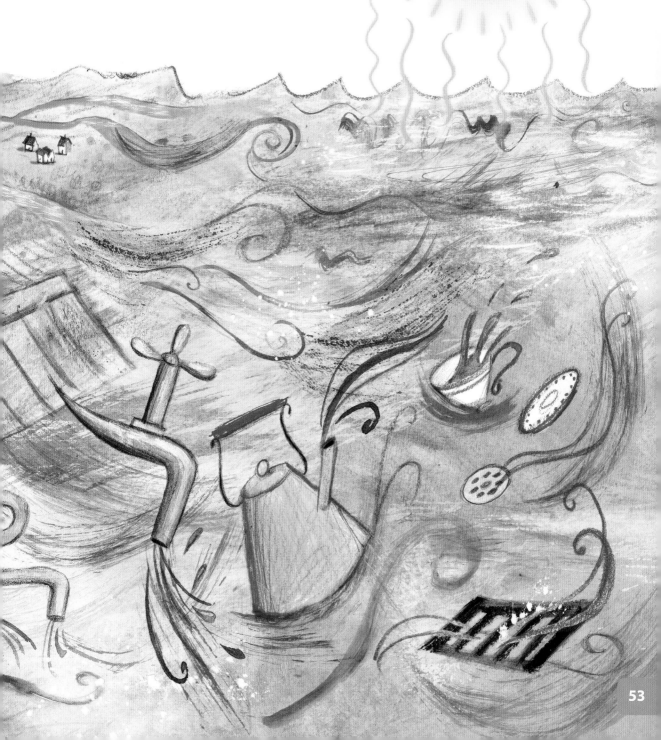

Where Does Water Come From?

Hello and welcome to Junior Science Challenge! Our question tonight is: "Where does water come from?"

I think it comes from clouds in the sky.

Sam

No, it comes from under the ground.

Ahmed

I say it comes from rivers and lakes.

Leila

Hmmm. From the sea?

Over to Professor Tapp. Who's right?

Jack

Water comes from all these different places! Let me explain.

The air cools and some water vapour turns back into tiny drops of water, becoming clouds. This change, from a gas back to a liquid, is called **condensation**.

The tiny water drops join together and get bigger. The clouds get too heavy and burst, so rain falls.

Warm winds and the heat of the sun act like a giant hair dryer. They cause some water in the sea to turn into a gas, **water vapour**. This change is called **evaporation**.

Some rain sinks into the ground. It comes back to the surface through wells or springs. The rest of the rain spills into lakes and rivers, which flow into the sea.

Glossary

condensation – when water vapour (warm gas) cools down and turns back to water (the opposite of evaporation)

evaporation – when water heats up enough to turn into a warm gas

water vapour – warm gas

As you can see, this whole process has no real beginning or end. It's like a wheel. That's why we call it...

THE WATER-CYCLE!

Smash and Grab!

John Dougherty

The sky was the brightest blue, and the air was hot and hazy. Adil wondered how Katie could pedal so energetically on a day like that.

"Come on, slowcoach!" she yelled over her shoulder, hurtling like a rocket down the hill. "The museum closes soon, and you're the one with the half-term history project!"

The wide flat parkland of Saxton Manor Museum lay below them, **encircled by its high stone wall**. Adil was used to the **congestion and bustle** of London; it felt strange to be able to see so far, and to see no other living soul except for his cousin.

Through the gates they sped, and along the winding driveway. Bees buzzed gently from flower to flower.

As they rounded the corner, something curious caught Adil's eye. "What's that weird box?" he asked, slowing to look at it.

"Careful!" Katie warned.

Adil pulled on the brakes, surprised at her sharp tone.

"It's a beehive," she explained. "And you were heading straight for its front door. There's always a guard bee on duty." She squinted curiously. "The bees look agitated. Better keep away."

They moved on to the museum entrance.

"Is there a guard here, too?" Adil joked as they entered.

"That's odd," Katie said. "There should be. Well, not a guard; but Mum's friend Mrs McCreevy should be here, selling the admission tickets."

"What's that hammering noise?" Adil wondered.

It came from a nearby door. A set of keys dangled from the lock, quivering with each blow.

"Hello?" Katie called.

"Help!" an anxious voice responded from the other side of the door.

"It's Mrs McCreevy!" Katie gasped, and she hurried to unlock it.

"Oh, thank goodness, Katie!" Mrs McCreevy said, when she saw who it was. "Someone locked me in the store-room! Did you see anyone leave?"

Katie shrugged. "We haven't seen anyone," she said.

"Not since we cycled down the hill," Adil added.

"Then whoever it was hasn't had time to get away," Mrs McCreevy said firmly. "Let's see if anything's missing."

The rooms on the ground floor seemed untouched. They hurried up the **magnificent marble staircase**.

"Oh, my!" Mrs McCreevy exclaimed, as they entered the first room upstairs. Three of the glass display cabinets had been smashed.

"What's missing?" Adil asked, looking round. The cabinets were full of military uniforms and equipment that had belonged to the Saxton family.

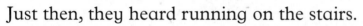

"Old Mr Richard's army greatcoat," Mrs McCreevy said, baffled. "A World War One flying helmet and gloves. And a World War Two gas mask. Why would anyone take them? They're valueless."

Just then, they heard running on the stairs.

"Hello?" came a voice. "It's the police! Sergeant Pemberton!"

Mrs McCreevy paled. "But that means… Oh, no! Quickly!"

The children, perplexed, hurried after Mrs McCreevy as she **ran breathlessly** up another flight of stairs after Sergeant Pemberton. As they entered a small room, she let out a shriek at the sight of four broken display cases. All were empty.

"An alarm at the police station went off when these cases were smashed," Sergeant Pemberton explained to the puzzled children.

"They contained the Saxton family jewellery," Mrs McCreevy added sombrely.

"The thief hasn't had time to get away," Adil reminded her.

"There are police cars at all the exits," Sergeant Pemberton said. "And five of my colleagues are searching the museum."

"So the thief will still be here," said Katie.

When they returned downstairs, five police officers were in the hallway with three other people. There was a red-faced man who was complaining very loudly, a pretty young woman, and a grumpy-looking older lady.

"We've searched them all," said a WPC. "None of them has any jewellery. Is anything else missing?"

"An army greatcoat, a flying helmet and gloves, and a gas mask," said Mrs McCreevy.

"Well, you can see I'm not hiding those!" snapped the red-faced man, crossing his arms angrily.

"That goes for all of us," smiled the pretty woman, rubbing at a red mark on her throat.

The grumpy-looking lady scowled.

"Well," said Sergeant Pemberton, "I'm afraid you'll have to wait here while we search the grounds."

The children followed him outside. "We'll help," they offered.

It wasn't long before Katie spotted something in the stream. She fished it out with a stick.

"It's the greatcoat!" Sergeant Pemberton exclaimed. "Well done, Katie. I bet the thief used it to conceal the jewellery."

But the coat was empty. Sergeant Pemberton waded into the stream and found the gloves, helmet, and gas mask, but nothing else.

"Bizarre," he said. "Why would the thief steal these and throw them away?"

An idea fizzed like shaken lemonade inside Adil's brain. "Maybe he'd finished using them!"

"Using them for what?" asked Katie.

Adil nodded towards the beehive. "Protection," he said.

"Of course!" Katie agreed. "That's why the bees were so agitated!"

Sergeant Pemberton grinned. "Adil, you're a genius." He pulled on the soggy greatcoat, helmet, gloves and gas mask. "Here goes," he said, stepping towards the beehive. The bees swarmed about him like tiny, furious helicopters as he lifted the top off and reached inside, but the bulky clothing kept him safe from their stings. He pulled out a thin bag and tossed it to the children.

It was full of jewellery.

Sergeant Pemberton closed up the beehive and turned back to them.

Only then did Katie notice a gap between his collar and the gas mask. "You're lucky you didn't get stung," she told him.

"It was worth the risk," he said. "Now, how can we tell who the thief is?"

"Maybe," Adil suggested, "the thief will give himself away when we show them that we've found the jewellery?"

The thief was clearly a good actor. None of the suspects looked guilty. The red-faced man shouted; the pretty woman smiled and rubbed the sore spot on her throat; the grumpy lady scowled.

"Well, Adil," Sergeant Pemberton murmured. "You worked out where the jewellery was. Any idea which of these people is the thief?"

Adil shook his head.

But now it was Katie's turn to have an idea fizz into her head. She walked over to the pretty young woman and looked up at her.

"Excuse me," she said, "but how did you get that bee-sting on your neck?"

WANTED
A New Planet!

Goodbye Earth?

Scientists believe Earth has been our home for around 200,000 years. Can we continue to live on Earth forever, though?

- The Earth is getting more and more crowded each year.

- As the population grows, more fuel is needed – oil, gas and coal. These fuels are running out.

- Some people think that if recent climate changes continue, many areas will become too hot to grow food. Also ocean levels could rise, flooding towns on the coasts.

- Some people believe that a meteor struck the Earth 65 million years ago, killing off most living creatures. If this happened again and we were living on another planet, we would survive.

For all these reasons, some scientists believe we may need to find a new planet to live on.

What we would need in our new home

Anywhere we moved to would need:

- *Oxygen*
  On Earth we get this from plants and trees, so we would need suitable land to grow them.

- *Water*
  This is vital to keep all living things alive.

- *The right temperature*
  Planets close to the sun are too hot for us, while those far away are too cold.

- *An energy source*
  We would need a fuel such as coal or oil, or a way of using lots of natural energy, such as the wind, to give us power.

- *Gravity*
  This would need to be about the same as the Earth's gravity.

Jupiter   Mars   Earth   Venus   Mercury   Sun

Life on Mars

Scientists have researched the idea of humans living on Mars for many years. In June 2010 six astronauts began a simulated mission to Mars, to see how they would cope with the long journey.

They lived in an imitation spacecraft for 520 days, though it never left the ground. During their 'trip' they ate food similar to that on a space station. They eventually 'landed' on 4 November 2011.

The astronauts did a simulated space walk on 'planet Mars'.

Unmanned spaceships and satellites have already been sent to Mars. Research suggests that there are large amounts of ice trapped underground. Many scientists believe that there was once life on Mars.

The unmanned spaceship, Phoenix, landed on Mars in 2008 to explore the planet.

What would we need to do to make Mars habitable again?

- The average surface temperature on Mars is minus 60 degrees Celsius. We would need to use gases to warm up the atmosphere to around 5 degrees Celsius.
- This would melt the large amounts of ice beneath the surface, with the water forming rivers and lakes.
- Introducing microbes to the soil would eventually produce enough oxygen to allow plants to grow.
- Plants would then give out oxygen to support human life.

There are some scientists who think this could be achieved in 100 years. Others think that the atmosphere on Mars could never support life, or that it would take thousands or even millions of years.

Animals in space

We need to know how animals would behave in space. This is because they would need to spend years in spaceships to get to their new home. Would they be able to survive and reproduce?

To find out, creatures have been sent into space. Experiments have used: fruitflies, monkeys, mice, dogs, rabbits, fish, frogs, spiders, tortoises, jellyfish and scorpions.

Almost all of the creatures survived their trip. Scientists also discovered that:

- Fish tended to swim in loops instead of in straight lines.

- Rats with broken bones took much longer to heal.
- Jellyfish born in zero gravity in space were able to tell up from down in their water. On Earth they can't.

If we were to grow flowering plants on another planet, we would need insects to pollinate them. In 1984, the space shuttle Challenger took 3,000 honey bees into space. They behaved normally and built honeycombs just the same as on Earth.

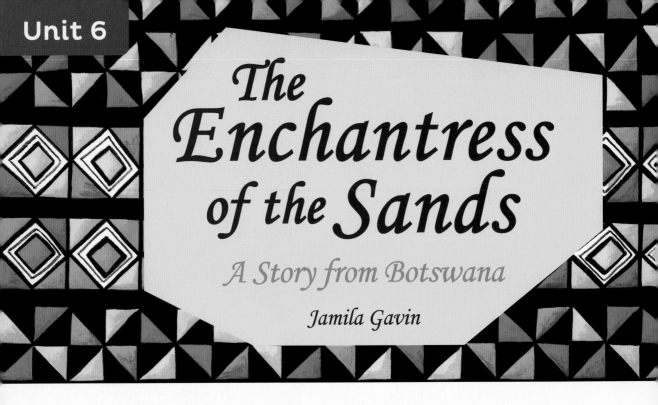

The Enchantress of the Sands

A Story from Botswana

Jamila Gavin

On the far side of the Singing Sands, where the sound of one step upon the shining white grains can be heard a hundred miles away, lived an evil **enchantress** who liked to steal children.

It was because of this enchantress that a desert **herdsman** decided to build a tree house for his three young motherless sons.

He built it high in the branches of an acacia tree, and the only way up or down was by a rope ladder.

Every day, the herdsman warned his sons, "While I'm away, don't let down the ladder to anyone except me. You will know when I come, for I will whistle three times."

The boys promised. So every day, when their father herded his cattle into the desert to graze, the boys would scamper about among the branches, happy as can be. And every evening, they let down

the rope ladder when they heard their father whistle.

But one day the evil enchantress came and sat in the deep shade of the acacia tree. She knew that above her head, three pairs of eyes gazed down at her.

"Little boys," she croaked, "let down the ladder so I can come up and see your wonderful tree house." But because they did not hear the whistle, the boys did not let down the ladder.

The wicked enchantress hid. The next evening when the father came home she heard him whistle three times, and down tumbled the ladder.

"Aha!" the enchantress gloated. "That's what I'll do!"

The boys told their father about the old woman. "Beware," he said. "It could have been the wicked enchantress of the Singing Sands."

The next day, when their father had gone into the desert, the enchantress came back. She whistled three times. Down came the ladder and the enchantress climbed up.

"Now I've got you!" she screamed, and tucking two boys under one arm and one under the other, she made off.

When the herdsman came home, he saw the dangling ladder.

He knew that something terrible had happened. The tree house was empty and his little boys gone. He thought his heart would break. He ran, howling, into the desert. "Has anyone seen my boys?"

The father ran to the door of a wise man and fell at his feet. "Help me, help me! My three sons have disappeared. I fear they may have been stolen by the wicked enchantress of the Singing Sands. What shall I do?"

"There is only one way to get them back, and that is to kill the enchantress. The only way to kill her is to break her magic stick in which all her powers lie. There is only one way to cross the Singing Sands without her hearing you, and that is to take my golden drum and beat it with this stick," the wise man said.

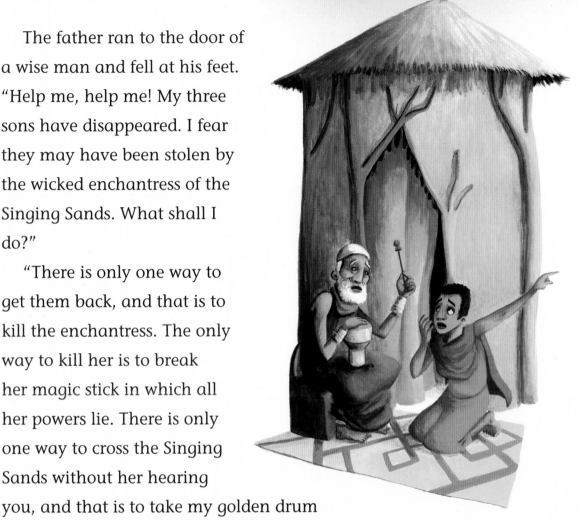

The herdsman rubbed ash in his hair to make it grey, and hid the golden drum under a cloak. Disguised as an old man, he set off towards the Singing Sands.

When he got to that shining white place, before he put one foot upon the sands, he began to beat the magic drum. As soft as a heartbeat, he crossed the Singing Sands.

On the other side he saw the enchantress's hut. He hobbled up to her door. "Oh! My aching stomach! Would a kind person have a crumb of food for a starving old man?"

"I didn't hear you coming," screamed the enchantress. "**Begone**!" But then she caught a glimpse of the golden drum beneath his cloak. She wanted it. "On second thoughts…" She gave a crocodile smile. "I may have a morsel left over. Come on in."

There was a cauldron bubbling, and the enchantress stirred it with her magic stick. Glowing in a dark corner were three pairs of frightened eyes, and the herdsman knew he had found his boys.

"Mmm! That smells good," he said, putting his nose into the steam.

"You can taste some when I've mixed in this powder," said the enchantress, thinking she could poison the old man and steal his drum. For a moment, she set down her magic stick to sprinkle in the poison. In that instant, the herdsman snatched up the stick and snapped it across his knee. The enchantress screamed, but before she could say a word, she crumbled into a pile of dust.

The herdsman joyfully hugged his sons and led them back across the shining white Singing Sands. He didn't bother to beat the golden drum. Everyone heard them coming and **rejoiced**.

Biography

Jamila Gavin: her childhood

by Charlotte Raby

She never thought she would be a writer

You may know Jamila Gavin as a children's writer who has written over 40 books set in many different times and places but she never thought she would be a writer when she was younger.

Jamila Gavin says that her childhood made her into a storyteller. She says that the boasts and exaggerations she made up about herself as an Indian girl in an English Primary school, St Saviour's school in Putney, were the beginning of her storytelling and eventually helped her to become the writer she is today.

Always on the move...

Jamila Gavin was born on 9 August 1941, in Mussoorie in the foothills of the Himalayas. Her father and mother were both teachers and they met in Iran. Soon after they married, they moved back to her father's country, India, and Jamila was born there. By the time she was 12, Jamila had lived in a Punjab Palace in India, a bombed-out street in Shepherd's Bush in London, a bungalow in Poona, which is near Mumbai, and a terraced house in Ealing, London.

Making friends

As Jamila moved many times as a child, she had to become good at making new friends. This is when she started to exaggerate things to interest her new friends. She would weave stories about the palace she had lived in and the tiger's footprints she had seen to enthral the other children. She also used these tales to explain her background because having an Indian father meant she looked very different to the other children.

Finally, after much toing and froing between India and England, Jamila's family settled in England. Jamila was 12 years old and it was 1953. She was sent to a private girls' school, The Girls' High School in Ealing. Jamila hated it. She was naughty and rebellious. In fact, she leapt for joy when she passed her end-of-school exams and left.

Autobiography

Out of India
by Jamila Gavin

Chapter 1
Boasting

I used to boast about many things when I was a child, especially on the occasions that we came over to England from India — three times before I was eleven years old — and each time I had to start making friends all over again in a new school. So when I was asked questions about myself in the different school playgrounds I got to know, it would often go as follows:

Q: *"Where do you come from?"*

A: **"India."**

I knew they thought of tigers and elephants and monkeys and fakirs sleeping on beds of nails.

Q: *"Where were you born?"*

A: **"In the Himalayas."**

That impressed them. They imagined my mother giving birth to me on the icy slopes of Mount Everest some twenty-nine thousand feet up, when in fact I was born about six thousand feet up in the Community Hospital, Landour, Mussoorie which was in the foothills of the Himalayas.

Autobiography

Q: *"Did you live in a mud hut?"*

Most people used to think that because India had so much poverty, everyone lived in a mud hut. First of all, in real poverty, you don't live in a mud hut but in a hovel made up of rags or sticks, or you are a pavement dweller and have nothing but a scrap of material. Secondly, mud huts may sound primitive, but they can be perfect dwelling places and ecologically, superbly efficient. In village India, which is where most people still live in such dwellings, they are kept beautifully clean and with a sense of pride. But even if a large number of people live in so-called mud huts — at one time, India was eighty per cent agricultural, there are now hundreds of towns and cities in which people live in homes made of bricks and mortar and stone and glass and concrete. In fact, it is sometimes hard to know if you are in Bombay or Los Angeles.

But me, I boasted:

A: **"I lived in a palace."**

This was true — although it wasn't exactly Buckingham Palace. It was a palace designed by an Italian for a Sikh prince, Sher Singh, some two hundred years ago and then abandoned.

It was deserted with a huge, wild, overgrown garden with mango and banana trees, and snakes in the grass and a water tank full of frogs and huge high pillars and terraces where wild bees made enormous bee hives which hung like buzzing sacks.

I think there must have been pomegranates too, because the palace was called 'Anarkali', meaning pomegranate.

Autobiography

Q: *"Have you ever seen a tiger?"*

I may have been a boaster, but I wasn't a liar, and to this day, I can't say that I have. But I still managed to make it sound glamorous and dangerous.

A: "Not exactly, but I've seen its footprints in the mud and followed it all along the banks of the Brahmaputra River, and I've seen the long grass crushed where it has just lain, and I've seen the remains of its dinner still fresh, and known that it was not far away — maybe even watching us."